DATE DUE

J
796.962
Ade

T 59814

Secrets, statistics, and little-known facts about hockey

Bruce Adelson

illustrations by Harry Pulver Jr.

Lerner Publications Company • Minneapolis

2-23-99 Lerner 23.93

For Sharon Craig, Vicki Fagliarone, Laurie Goss, Sally Keyes, Jan McConnel, and Lorraine Hasiatka—second grade teachers at Zachary Taylor Elementary School in Arlington, Virginia. Your dedication, collegiality, and professionalism will inspire me for years to come. Thank you.

—B.A.

Thank you to Craig Campbell, Assistant Manager/Resource Center and Jane Rodney of the Hockey Hall of Fame in Toronto, Ontario, for their help and camaraderie while I was researching this book. The assistance of Chris Cistero, Christian Ficara, Justin Fricke, Larry Kinkle, and Charles Wheeler of Joan Yocum's fifth grade language arts class at Zachary Taylor Elementary School is gratefully acknowledged. Your exuberance and helpful review of this book contributed to its completion. Thanks as well to Joan Yocum, whose enthusiasm for our writing project will always be appreciated.

Illustrations by Harry Pulver Jr.
Book design and electronic prepress: Steve Foley, Mike Kohn, Steve Schweitzer, Sean Todd

This book is available in two editions:
Library binding by Lerner Publications Company
Soft cover by First Avenue Editions
241 First Avenue North, Minneapolis, MN 55401

Copyright © 1999 Bruce Adelson

All rights reserved. International copyright secured. No part of this book may be reproduced or transmitted in any form or by any means, electronic or mechanical, including photocopying and recording, or by any information storage or retrieval system, without permission in writing from Lerner Publications Company, except for the inclusion of brief quotations in an acknowledged review.

Library of Congress Cataloging-in-Publication Data

Adelson, Bruce.
   Hat trick trivia / by Bruce Adelson ; illustrations by Harry Pulver, Jr.
     p. cm.
   Includes bibliographical references and index.
   Summary: Presents facts and figures about the game of hockey—past and present, and particularly about professional play in the NHL.
   ISBN 0-8225-3315-4 (hardcover : alk. paper). — ISBN 0-8225-9806-X (paperback : alk. paper)
   1. Hockey—Miscellanea—Juvenile literature. 2. Hockey—Records—Juvenile literature. [1. Hockey—Mixcellanea.] I. Pulver, Harry, ill. II. Title.
GV847.25.A34   1999
796.962—dc21   97–48485

Manufactured in the United States of America
1 2 3 4 5 6 - JR - 04 03 02 01 00 99

Contents

1 The Game of Hockey 6

2 Black Hockey Players 22

3 Women and Hockey 28

4 Statistics 38

5 Hockey's Best Players 48

Trivia Teaser Answers *54*

Resources to Check Out *60*

Hat Trick Bibliography *61*

Index *63*

About the Author and Illustrator *64*

Chapter 1

The Game of Hockey

Did You Know?

The earliest evidence of a hockey game comes from a seventeenth century painting by Dutch artist Hendrick Avercamp. In the painting, called *Winter Landscape,* there is a scene of several men skating on a patch of ice, chasing a small white ball with sticks.

Detail from Winter Landscape

In the seventeenth and eighteenth centuries, Dutch and English settlers in New England, New York, and eastern Canada, played a game on ice that very much resembled hockey. Ice hockey began as a sport similar to land games like shinty, shinny, lacrosse, and bandy. The word "hockey" comes from the French word *hoquet,* meaning a crook or stick, used by shepherds to herd flocks of sheep or other animals.

Although hockey is played in many countries around the world, it is the national sport of Canada. Canadians have always been at the forefront in making hockey the world-class sport it has become.

The earliest hockey games were not like modern ones. There were often seven players on each team. In modern games, a team has six players on the ice at a time—one goalie, two defenders, one right wing, one left wing, and one center. Centers and wings are also called forwards.

Early games were not played according to any standard set of rules. On March 3, 1875, the first organized game of hockey with rules was played in Montreal, a city in the Canadian province of Quebec. This game also featured the first flat puck in hockey history. The puck was made of wood.

Seven-player teams at Montreal's Victoria Rink around 1893

Trivia Teaser #1

What is the Stanley Cup?

Did You Know?

The flat puck was invented one night in nineteenth century Canada. Indoor games then were played at the Victoria Rink in Montreal. The rubber ball used by the players was always bouncing and hopping off the ice, breaking windows and causing other damage. The rink owners had spent hundreds of dollars for repairs.

The ice rink manager became tired of seeing hockey balls bouncing all over the arena. He also may have been tired of sweeping up glass from broken windows. He decided to change things. The next time the ball bounced into the stands, the manager picked it up and with his knife, cut off two round slabs from opposite ends of the ball. He tossed the flat, center part of the ball onto the rink's ice. The game started again, with the players using their new, flat puck. They preferred it to the round ball since it slid along the ice, could be easily passed and did not bounce out of play. From then on, flat pucks were used in all ice hockey games. Modern hockey pucks are made of vulcanized rubber.

What is the oldest piece of equipment used by a hockey player?

Until that game in Montreal, hockey was played with different kinds of roundish objects—apples, pieces of coal and balls like those used in lacrosse. Round pucks are harder to control than flat ones because they bounce instead of sliding along the ice. A bouncing ball–puck is also more likely to fly into the seats and hit a fan than a flat puck is.

Did You Know?

Hockey's earliest games were played outdoors in Canada during the winter. Before refrigeration was invented, the cold wintry air was needed to keep the ice frozen. But the cold temperatures caused many unusual problems. The referees, for example, used metal whistles to signal penalties and to stop the game. Sometimes, the weather during a game was so cold that the whistles froze to the referees' lips. Games had to be stopped so the whistles could be removed. To avoid this problem, referees started using hand bells, like the ones school teachers had. But some fans brought their own bells to games and rang them to confuse the opposing team's players. All of these problems were solved with the invention of plastic whistles, which did not stick to referees' lips.

Many of the first hockey sticks were wooden handles from farm plows and saplings that players cut down and carved into sticks. Today's hockey sticks are lighter and easier to handle than the old wooden plow handles. Modern sticks also are coated with a substance called kevlar. Kevlar makes sticks strong and rigid and therefore less likely to break.

Until the 1950s, hockey stick blades had to be straight. Andy Bathgate of the New York Rangers is believed to be the first player to use a bent blade. In the early 1950s, Bathgate discovered that he could shoot harder and make the puck dip while it was in flight if he bent his straight hockey stick blade. Soon other players experimented with bent blades, looking for the best angle for different types of shots. When you watch a National Hockey League (NHL) game, you will notice that most players' sticks have some type of bend or curve in the blade.

Q: *When was the first professional hockey league formed?*

A: *The International Hockey League was formed with teams from Canada and the United States in 1904.* After that league folded others cropped up. In 1917 the National Hockey Association and the Pacific Coast League joined to form the National Hockey League, which remains the world's highest level of play.

The role of goalie has probably changed more than that of any other player on a hockey team. A modern goalie—with heavy leg pads, a fancy mask, glove, wide stick, and a pad on the arm called a blocker—doesn't look anything like goalies did in the past.

Goalies did not wear leg pads until 1924. Before that, many goaltenders stuffed stocking caps down the front of their hockey pants for protection against flying pucks. Goalies also had to stand up the entire game. They were expected to block shots while standing. Diving or falling onto the ice to stop pucks from going into the net was against the rules. Early goalies had to use the same narrow sticks that the other players used. They also did not wear face masks.

Did You Know?

A woman was the first hockey player to wear a face mask during an organized hockey game. Elizabeth Graham was the goalie for the Queens University women's hockey team in Canada. In 1927 she decided to wear a wire fencing mask to protect her face during games.

Trivia Teaser #3

"I always wanted to be a goalie. When I was two years old, my mom says I used to throw rolled-up socks up the stairs and stop them when they came back down. I guess being a goalie was in my blood. The biggest misconception about being a goaltender is that you don't have to skate and the kid that skates the worst goes in the net. That is not the case. To be a good goaltender, you need to be good on your feet. You need to be able to skate and move around. If you have great reflexes and can't skate, you're not going to be a goalie."

WHO AM I?

Clint Benedict

Clint Benedict played professional hockey for 18 years. After having his nose broken by a puck in a game, he became the first pro goalie to wear a mask in 1930. Benedict wore the mask, made of leather with a large space for his nose, for one game. He didn't like the mask—he said the nosepiece was so big he couldn't see around it. He never used it again.

Benedict was also the first goalie to drop to his knees when blocking shots. He influenced the NHL to change its rules to allow goalies to do this. Clint Benedict is a member of hockey's Hall of Fame.

Goalies did not begin to use masks regularly until the late 1950s. Jacques *(ZHANK)* Plante, goalie for the Montreal Canadiens, began wearing his on November 1, 1959, during a game against the New York Rangers. After a puck cut his nose, Plante needed stitches. When he went back into the game, he decided to wear a mask to protect his injury.

At that time, fans were not used to seeing goalies wear face masks. They thought Plante looked funny when he put his on, so they laughed. They stopped laughing when Plante made several big saves and helped Montreal win the game.

Plante later became well known for designing his own masks. But it was not until 1962, when Terry Sawchuck began using a mask regularly, that face masks became accepted as part of a goalie's uniform. Jacques Plante and Terry Sawchuck are members of the Hockey Hall of Fame.

Over the years, masks have changed a lot. Early masks were solid pieces of material, with slots for the eyes, nose, and mouth. Modern masks have shields much like cages in front to protect the face. These masks allow goalies to see better than earlier models did.

Modern face masks are also very colorful, unlike the early masks, which were basically white or tan. Masks are often painted with the colors of the goalie's team. But sometimes, special things can be painted on them. During the 1970s, Gerry Cheevers played goalie for the Boston Bruins. Every time a puck hit his mask during practice, he painted stitches on it to show the injuries he avoided by wearing his face mask.

Over the years, hockey became an ever quicker game, as players continued to skate faster and shoot pucks harder

John Vanbiesbrouk

Gerry Cheevers

than those who had played before them. Two of hockey's most famous skaters and scorers were Bobby Hull and Maurice Richard. Richard was one of hockey's fastest skaters when he played for the Montreal Canadiens in the 1950s and 1960s. Nicknamed the Rocket because of his speed, he was one of hockey's greatest scorers. On March 18, 1945, Richard became the first NHL player to score 50 goals in one season.

Maurice Richard scores another goal.

Trivia Teaser #4

During the 1984–85 season, I became only the third rookie in NHL history to record 100+ points (43 goals and 57 assists) in one season. I am also the only player besides Wayne Gretzky to score 200+ points in one season. I did this in 1989. In the 1995–96 season, I scored more goals than any other NHL player. I played for the Pittsburgh Penguins. WHO AM I?

Bobby Hull was nicknamed the Golden Jet. He had blonde hair and skated very fast, like a jet. During his NHL career with the Chicago Blackhawks in the 1960s and 1970s, Hull was known for having hockey's hardest shot. He could shoot pucks at about 100 miles per hour. Hall of Fame goalie Jacques Plante faced Bobby Hull many times during his career. Commenting on Hull's slapshot, Plante once said, "It's like being hit by a piece of lead. You have to see it coming to believe it."

Bobby Hull scored more than 1,000 goals in his professional hockey career with Chicago and with the Hartford Whalers of the NHL and the Winnipeg Jets of the World Hockey Association (WHA). (The WHA was a pro hockey league that is no longer in business.)

Only three players have scored at least 1,000 goals in professional hockey—Bobby Hull, Wayne Gretzky, and Gordie Howe. Bobby Hull, Gordie Howe, and Maurice Richard are members of hockey's Hall of Fame. Bobby Hull's son, Brett, plays for the St. Louis Blues. When he scored his 500th career goal in 1996, Brett and Bobby became the first father-son combination in history to score 500 goals each in their NHL careers.

Bobby and Brett Hull look happy after Brett scored his 50th goal—not knowing there would be so many more to come.

Q: Which National Hockey League goalie was the first to score a goal by shooting the puck into the other team's net?

A. Ron Hextall

B. Patrick Roy (WHAH)

C. John Vanbiesbrouck

D. Mike Richter

Turn the page for the answer.

A: **A. Ron Hextall of the Philadelphia Flyers.** On December 8, 1987, Hextall became the first NHL goalie to score a goal by shooting the puck into the other team's goal in a game against the Boston Bruins. He is also the first NHL goalie to score a goal in a playoff game. He scored again on April 11, 1989, against the Washington Capitals. Hextall remembers the night he scored his first goal, "I told everybody I was going to score a goal eventually. It was just a matter of time. The first one, I just shot over everybody's head and it went in the net. It was fun. Our whole team congratulated me."

Trivia Teaser #5

What is a Zamboni machine and how did it get its unusual name?

Did You Know?

During the 1993 NHL All-Star Game, Al Iafrate of the Washington Capitals was credited with having the hardest, fastest slapshot in history. In a pregame exhibition, Iafrate's shot was clocked at 105.2 miles per hour.

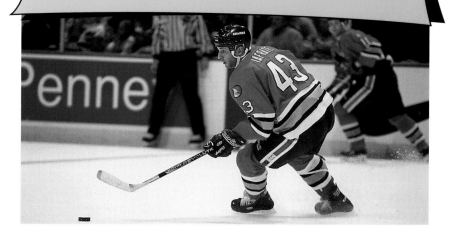

There are three periods in a National Hockey League game. How long does each period last ?

A. 30 minutes   C. 20 minutes
B. 1 hour   D. 45 minutes

C. Each period is 20 minutes long. During the regular season, there can be one overtime period of 5 minutes if the game is tied after the three periods are over. During the playoffs, overtime continues until one team scores.

Chapter 2

Black Hockey Players

Of North America's top four team sports—hockey, basketball, baseball, and football—hockey has seen the least participation of black athletes. Henry Beckett, an African American athlete, played college hockey at Springfield College in Massachusetts from 1903 to 1906. Charles Brooks played on a Medford, Massachusetts, team in 1938 and later practiced with the Boston Bruins.

It wasn't until the 1950s that black hockey players played in the National Hockey League. No league rule kept out black players. But compared to the large number of white athletes who played hockey, very few black athletes had much interest in the sport. Willie O'Ree was an exception to that rule.

Willie O'Ree

O'Ree was born in Fredericton, New Brunswick, a province in eastern Canada, and he loved playing hockey. As a young boy, he dreamed of someday playing in the National Hockey League. When he was a teenager, O'Ree was a good athlete. He was offered a contract to play professional baseball by the Boston Braves. Instead, he wanted to play hockey. In 1956, Willie signed his first pro hockey contract with a Canadian team, the Quebec Aces.

In 1958, his dream came true when the Boston Bruins brought him to the NHL for a game against the Montreal Canadiens. He played his first game for the Bruins on January 18, 1958, at the Montreal Forum. After playing a couple of seasons in the minor leagues, he played in 43 games for Boston in the 1960–61 season. After that season, he played 19 more years in the minor leagues.

Trivia Teaser #6

I was the first black man to play goalie for a National Hockey League team when I began my career with the Edmonton Oilers in 1981. With Edmonton in 1984, I also became the first black goaltender to win a Stanley Cup championship. Later I became the goaltender for the St. Louis Blues.
WHO AM I?

Willie O'Ree did not have an easy career. He was often discriminated against because he was black. Some fans did not want O'Ree to play hockey with white players because of his skin color. During one game, someone threw a black hat onto the ice to make fun of him. Some players also taunted him. "But," O'Ree said, "it went in one ear and out the other."

Although Willie O'Ree's career helped other blacks follow him into the National Hockey League, the number of black hockey players has remained small.

Since O'Ree's career ended, only a couple dozen black men have played in the NHL. Alton White, born in the Canadian province of Nova Scotia, played for the Los Angeles Sharks in 1973, becoming the second black athlete in professional hockey. Val James, an African American hockey player from Florida, played in the Eastern Hockey League and in the American Hockey League in the 1970s.

Did You Know?

The longest professional hockey game in history lasted 5 hours and 51 minutes. Detroit and Montreal began the game the evening of March 24, 1936. The game ended on at 2:25 the following morning. A Detroit player named Mud Bruneteau scored the only goal of the game in the sixth overtime period. Back then, teams played overtime periods until someone scored a goal to break the tie.

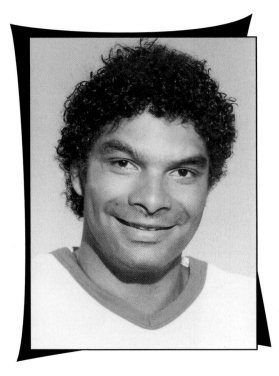

Tony McKegney

During the 1978–79 season, Tony McKegney began his NHL career with the Buffalo Sabres. Born in Montreal, McKegney played left wing. In 14 seasons in the NHL, he played in 912 games, scored 320 goals, with 319 assists and 639 total points, the most by any black man in NHL history. Like Willie O'Ree, McKegney also experienced racism. In one game, the opposing team's goalie taunted McKegney, yelling racial insults.

Grant Fuhr, goalie for the St. Louis Blues, began his hockey career in the 1980s. He was the first black goaltender in NHL history. Anson Carter, center for the Washington Capitals, played first for Michigan State. In 1996, Mike Grier of the Edmonton Oilers became the first African American player in the NHL who was born and trained in the United States.

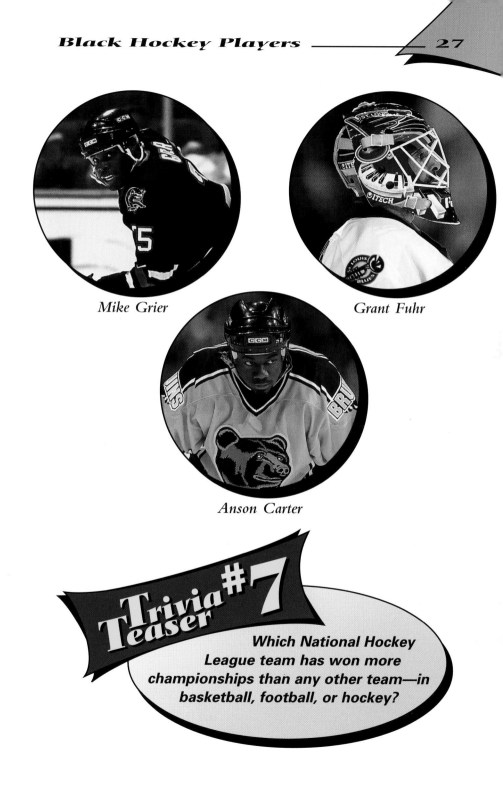

Mike Grier

Grant Fuhr

Anson Carter

Trivia Teaser #7

Which National Hockey League team has won more championships than any other team—in basketball, football, or hockey?

Chapter 3

Women and Hockey

In the late nineteenth century, Lord Stanley of Preston was the governor general of Canada. Lord Stanley, a big hockey fan, played an important role in developing women's hockey. Every winter, he made a rink on the lawn of the governor's mansion by flooding the grass with water, which turned to ice. Lord Stanley and Lady Stanley played hockey along with their eight sons and two daughters. Family friends visited to play on the rink, too.

Lord Stanley

Women in long skirts played hockey at Rideau Hall in Ottawa. Lord Stanley's daughter, Isobel, is in white.

Lord Stanley's daughter Isobel was one of Canada's earliest hockey players. In 1889, she played for Government House against a team called the Rideau *(ree DOH)* Ladies in what is thought to have been the first women's hockey game.

After that first game, women's hockey spread across Canada. Teams were formed at many universities. In 1900 the first women's hockey league was founded in Quebec, Canada. Most games were played outside. For uniforms, players wore skirts, heavy sweaters and stocking caps. When these women's teams played, no fans were allowed to watch the games. At that time, many people thought women should not be allowed to play a rough sport like hockey. It was also considered impolite to allow male spectators to watch women playing sports. The only people at these games besides the players were a referee and two judges.

The varsity women's hockey team at the University of Toronto holds practice.

The early 1900s saw some very talented teams and intense rivalries. The Preston Rivulettes *(riv yoo LETS)*—perhaps the greatest women's hockey team in history—was formed in Canada in 1931. The Rivulettes won all but 2 of more than 350 games between 1930 and 1940 and won 10 straight championships in Canada.

The Preston Rivulettes, 1931-32 champions of the Ladies' Ontario Hockey Association. By this time, women had chucked the skirts in favor of real hockey gear.

During the 1940s and 1950s, interest in women's hockey dropped, in part due to World War II. Many players went to work during that time. In addition, men's and boys' hockey was booming, and women's teams had a hard time competing for ice time. Nonetheless, women's hockey did not disappear completely. A three-team league played in Montreal during the war years. One of its players, Hazel McCallion, was one of the first women ever to be paid for playing hockey. She got five dollars a game. McCallion, who later became the mayor of Mississauga, Ontario, has been a key supporter of women's hockey for many years.

A few teams survived in other parts of Canada as well. One of these, the Moose Jaw Wildcats from Saskatchewan, was forced to play outdoors after the Canadian army took over their arena for training purposes in the early 1940s. By the 1950s, with little competition around, the Wildcats played against men's teams.

Did You Know?

In 1955 Abby Hoffman registered—as Ab Hoffman—to play hockey in the Toronto Hockey League, which only had male players. No one realized Hoffman was a girl until officials checked her birth certificate after selecting her for an all-star team. The story made headlines across Canada. Hoffman was not allowed to play hockey the following year, so she took up swimming and track, becoming an Olympic medalist in 1972. She later was the director of Sport Canada in Ottawa.

Ab Hoffman poses with a figure-skating friend.

Women's hockey again blossomed in the 1960s. College teams flourished, as did youth house leagues. Women's amateur teams cropped up throughout Canada and the United

States. Tournaments, such as the Dominion Ladies Hockey Tournament, became annual events. The Dominion tournament started in 1967 with 22 teams in 3 divisions. By 1994 the tournament included 258 teams in 25 divisions.

A women's team in Montreal poses in 1962. Some of the players continued to wear figure skates.

When and where was the first official Women's World Championship hockey tournament held?

Ottawa, Ontario, hosted the first tournament sanctioned by the International Ice Hockey Federation (IIHF) in 1990. In 1987, the Ontario Women's Hockey Association held a smaller yet successful Women's World Hockey Tournament. The earlier event built enthusiasm for more international tournaments, including the IIHF tournament. The Women's World Championships are held every other year. Team Canada won the first four tournaments, in 1990, 1992, 1994, and 1996.

Manon Rheaume

Manon Rheaume *(ma NOH ray OHM)* is one of the most famous modern women hockey players. She was the goalie for the Canadian National Women's team that won the 1992 World Championship. After winning the championship, she was invited to training camp by the Tampa Bay Lightning of the National Hockey League.

Before the start of the 1993–94 NHL season, Rheaume became the first woman to play in a major league hockey game. She was Tampa Bay's goaltender during the first period of an exhibition game against the St. Louis Blues.

After that game, she signed a three-year contract with Tampa Bay. She was sent by the Lightning to play for the Atlanta Knights, a minor league hockey team in the International Hockey League. On December 13, 1993, Manon became the first woman goaltender to play in a reg-ular-season hockey game in a men's hockey league. She played in the second period against a team from Salt Lake City and gave up only one goal.

During the 1993–94 season, she was also the starting goalie for Nashville, a minor league hockey team that plays in the East Coast Hockey League. In 1994, Rheaume won another world championship as goaltender for Team Canada.

Canada's women's hockey team beat the U.S. team 4-3 in the 1997 Women's World Hockey Championship.

In 1998, women's hockey made its Olympic debut. As expected, Team Canada and Team USA were the strongest teams. In the championship game, the U. S. women's team thrilled its fans by beating Canada, 3–1, for the gold medal. As women's hockey has grown into a major intercollegiate sport, with world championships and a spot in the Olympic Games, more and more girls will have opportunities to watch and play the game.

The U.S. women's team celebrates winning the gold medal at the 1998 Olympics in Nagano, Japan.

Cammi Granato

 Who scored the first goal in the history of the United States women's Olympic ice hockey team?

A: **At the 1998 Winter Olympics in Nagano, Japan, Cammi Granato became the first woman to score a goal for the U.S. women's Olympic ice hockey team.** The 1998 Games were the first to include women's hockey. Cammi grew up playing hockey with her three brothers. Her older brother, Tony, went on to play for the San Jose Sharks in the National Hockey League. At the 1998 Olympics, Cammi was the captain of the U.S. team, which won the first gold medal ever awarded in the Olympics for women's ice hockey.

Chapter 4

Statistics

Goals, assists, and total points are three of hockey's most important statistics. When a player shoots the puck into the other team's net, he scores a goal. Players are given an assist if they pass the puck to a player who then scores a goal. One point is given for each assist and each goal. Total points are determined by adding a player's assists and goals.

Here is an example. Joe Sakic of the Colorado Avalanche has scored 285 goals and 461 assists in his NHL career.

$$\begin{array}{r} 285 \\ +461 \\ \hline 746 \end{array}$$

Q: Which player has scored more goals, has more assists and more total points than any other player in National Hockey League history?

A. Gordie Howe

B. Mario Lemieux

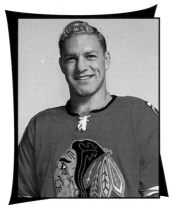

C. Bobby Hull

D. Wayne Gretzky

Turn the page for the answer.

A: **D. Wayne Gretzky holds every important NHL scoring record.** In the first 18 years of his NHL career, Gretzky had 837 goals, 1,771 assists and 2,608 points. If you add his goals and assists in the playoffs and in the World Hockey Association to these totals, you'll see that Gretzky has had more than 1,000 goals, 2,000 assists and 3,000 points in his career.

Trivia Teaser #8

Each year, the National Hockey League gives out awards to different players who have excelled at specific aspects of the game. Do you know which players are given the Vezina Trophy and the Art Ross Trophy?

Did You Know?

One of hockey's strangest games took place during the 1975 Stanley Cup Finals between the Philadelphia Flyers and Buffalo Sabres. The game was played in Buffalo's Memorial Auditorium, which had no air conditioning, so it could get very hot. During the game's second period, the temperature inside the auditorium was 86 degrees. It was so warm that fog formed as the hot air hit the cold ice. During the third period, players were waist deep in fog on the ice. The clouds and fog were so thick, the players couldn't find the puck. Every few minutes, the referee asked the players to skate quickly in circles to create breezes strong enough to blow away the fog. The game was stopped 12 times because the clouds were too thick for players to see. But fog was not the only thing that made this game strange. At one point, a bat started flying around the auditorium. It flew over the ice several times until one of the players knocked it out of the air with his hockey stick. After four hours, the Fog and Bat Game ended. Buffalo beat Philadelphia 5–4.

BUMP

 *True or false: When Wayne Gretzky became hockey's greatest goal scorer, he broke Gordie Howe's scoring record.*

True. Gordie Howe scored 801 goals in his National Hockey League career. Howe was the first NHL player to score 800 goals. He played professional hockey in five different decades, the 1940s, '50s, '60s, '70s and '80s. When he scored his 800th goal in 1980, Howe was a 51-year-old grandfather. Near the end of his career, Howe played for the Hartford Whalers—on the same team with his sons, Mark and Marty. Do you think your grandfather could do what Gordie Howe did?

Wayne Gretzky met Gordie Howe when he was 11 years old.

Did You Know?

Wayne Gretzky was the first NHL player to score 200 points in one season. In the 1981–82 season, he scored 212 points in 92 games while playing for the Edmonton Oilers.

Another key statistic is the average number of points a player scores in each game. This tells you how much a player contributes to his or her team each game by scoring goals or assisting teammates when they try to score. Take Wayne Gretzky for example. Between 1979 and 1998 he scored 2,795 points in 1,417 NHL games. To figure out Wayne's average, divide his points into his games like this:

$$2{,}795 \div 1{,}417 = 1.972477$$

Round this number off to two decimal places (the two numbers to the right of the decimal point) and you get 1.97. Scoring almost 2 points per game is excellent.

Mario Lemieux played 669 games and he scored 1,372 points in the NHL. Can you tell the average number of points Mario has scored in each game he has played?

    A. 2.01   B. 1.98

    C. 2.05   D. 2.15

C. Mario Lemieux scored 2.05 points per game in his National Hockey League career.

Mark Messier

Trivia Teaser #9

Mark Messier of the New York Rangers has 539 goals, 929 assists and 1,468 points in his NHL career. He has played 1,201 games. What is Mark's points-per-game average?

Hockey also has a statistic called +/− (plus-minus) points. Here is how to figure it out. All players on the ice when their team scores receive one + (plus) point. All players on the ice when their opponent scores receive one − (minus) point. This statistic is used to demonstrate how valuable players are to their teams by showing whether they help score and also whether they prevent opponents from scoring.

Here is an example of +/− points for one player in one game. Let's say the New York Rangers defeat the Pittsburgh Penguins 3–2. In that game, Wayne Gretzky of the Rangers was on the ice for all three of his team's goals so he receives three + points. He was on the ice for one of Pittsburgh's goals so he receives one − point. To figure out Wayne's total for this game, combine 3 + points and 1 − point like this:

$$\begin{array}{r} + \ 3 \\ - \ 1 \\ \hline + \ 2 \text{ points} \end{array}$$

The answer here is a + number because 3, a + number, is bigger than 1, a − number. The biggest number will decide whether your answer is a + or a −.

What if we reversed these numbers and gave Wayne 3 − points and 1 + point. How do we figure the +/− statistic for this game now?

$$\begin{array}{r} - \ 3 \\ + \ 1 \\ \hline - \ 2 \end{array}$$

Wayne would have 2 − points instead of + points because 3 is bigger than 1 and 3 is a − number.

Goals against average (GAA) is a statistic that measures how good a goaltender is. The GAA can tell you the average number of goals that a goalie allows the opposing team to score. This statistic is figured by multiplying the number of goals a goalie gives up by 60. Why 60? Sixty represents the number of minutes in an NHL game, which has 3 periods of 20 minutes each (20 x 3 = 60).

After multiplying these numbers, divide the result by the number of minutes the goalie played. Let's look at one example. In 1995–96, John Vanbiesbrouck of the Florida Panthers gave up 142 goals and played 3,178 minutes. The first step is to multiply:

$$\begin{array}{r} 142 \\ \underline{\times\ 60} \\ 8{,}520 \end{array}$$

Next step, divide:

$$8{,}520 \div 3{,}178 \text{ minutes} = 2.68$$

This is John's GAA. Any GAA less than 3.00 is excellent.

Trivia Teaser #10

What if Patrick Roy of the Colorado Avalanche gives up 165 goals in one season while playing 3,565 minutes. What is Patrick's goals against average?

Chapter 5

Hockey's Best Players

Over the years, the statistics of every National Hockey League player have been recorded. Here is a list of hockey's greatest players and some of their most important statistics. They are divided into five different categories that will tell you the top five players with the most goals, the most assists, the most total points, the most points per game, and best goals against average in hockey history. Some of the players in the league in the 1990s are also listed, so you can see how your favorites match up against the best players in hockey history. Your knowledge of hockey statistics will help you compare players.

SCORING

Most Goals Scored

Wayne Gretzky	837
Gordie Howe	801
Marcel Dionne	731
Phil Esposito	717
Mike Gartner	664

Players of the '90s

Wayne Gretzky	837
Mike Gartner	664
Jari Kurri	583
Mario Lemieux	563
Brett Hull	485

Marcel Dionne

Most Assists

Wayne Gretzky	1,771
Gordie Howe	1,049
Marcel Dionne	1,040
Paul Coffey	1,038
Ray Bourque	970

Players of the '90s

Wayne Gretzky	1,771
Paul Coffey	1,038
Ray Bourque	970
Mark Messier	929
Jaromir Jagr	319

Paul Coffey

Did You Know?

Lorne John Worsley had one of hockey's strangest nicknames. He was called Gump, because he looked like a popular Canadian cartoon character who had that name. Gump Worsley played for the New York Rangers, the Montreal Canadiens, and the Minnesota North Stars. His career spanned from 1952 to 1974. Worsley was short, heavy, and a little funny looking, but he was also one of the best goaltenders to ever play hockey. He is a member of the Hockey Hall of Fame.

Most Total Points

Wayne Gretzky	2,608
Gordie Howe	1,846
Marcel Dionne	1,771
Phil Esposito	1,590
Mark Messier	1,468

Points per Game

Wayne Gretzky	2.08
Mario Lemieux	2.05
Mike Bossy	1.50
Bobby Orr	1.39
Steve Yzerman	1.33

Players of the '90s

Wayne Gretzky	2,608
Mark Messier	1,468
Mario Lemieux	1,372
Dino Ciccarelli	1,103
Joe Sakic	746

Players of the '90s

Wayne Gretzky	2.08
Mark Messier	1.222
Jari Kurri	1.220
Dale Hawerchuk	1.209
Brian Leetch	1.009

Wayne Gretzky

Best Goals Against Average in a Single Season

George Hainsworth	0.92
George Hainsworth	1.05
Alex Connell	1.12
Clint Benedict	1.42
Wilf Cude	1.47

Players of the '90s

Dominik Hasek	1.95
Dominik Hasek	2.11
Ron Hextall	2.17
Jim Carey	2.26
Patrick Roy	2.36

Dominik Hasek

George Hainsworth

Trivia Teaser #11

Most hockey players in the National Hockey League have been Canadians. But there have also been many Americans. Who is the highest scoring American player in National Hockey League history?

Did You Know?

Bep Guidolin (GWID-o-lin) is the youngest person to ever play in a National Hockey League game. Bep was only 16 years old when he played his first NHL game for the Boston Bruins on November 12, 1942.

Trivia Teaser Answers

#1

Answer: The Stanley Cup is given each season to the champions of the National Hockey League. It weighs 32 pounds and is made of silver. The names of all players and teams that have won the Stanley Cup are inscribed into its silver coating. The cup is named for Lord Stanley of Preston. Lord Stanley purchased the cup for about $50 to honor the best hockey teams in Canada. The Montreal Hockey Club, an amateur team, won the first cup in 1893. Since 1910, the Stanley Cup has been awarded each year to the best professional hockey team.

Stanley Cup around 1920

Stanley Cup in 1997

This 1800s woodcut shows people ice skating.

Answer: Ice skates. The oldest discovered skates go back more than 3,000 years, to the twelfth century B.C. They were made from animal bones. There are old documents showing the first metal ice skate blades appearing in 1572. Early blades were attached to a piece of wood with leather straps. The front end of the blade was curved up over the skater's toes.

Answer: Ron Hextall. Hextall—goalkeeper for the Philadelphia Flyers from 1986 to 1993 and from 1994 to 1998—is an excellent skater and puckhandler. As a rookie first-string goalie in the 1986–87 season, he won the Vezina Trophy and was named a First Team All-Star.

#4 *Answer: Mario Lemieux.* Mario is one of the greatest scorers in the National Hockey League. During the 1988–89 season, Mario became the 7th player in NHL history to score 70 goals in one season. The next year, he scored 214 points. Wayne Gretzky is the only other NHL player to score at least 200 points in one season. Mario led the NHL with 69 goals in the 1995–96 season.

Zamboni

#5 *Answer: The Zamboni machine is used to resurface and refinish the ice—which is scraped and cracked by sticks and skate blades—between periods of hockey games.* The machine was invented by Frank Zamboni in the 1940s. Zamboni decided to name his invention after himself. The first Zamboni machine was used in 1949. Driven across the ice, the Zamboni lifts off snow and ice particles from the ice surface. It also applies a layer of water to smooth the surface. Before Mr. Zamboni introduced his invention, six men would take about 90 minutes to refinish a hockey rink's ice. Imagine how long hockey games would take today without the Zamboni machine.

#6

Answer: Grant Fuhr. Grant started his NHL career with the Edmonton Oilers. Born in the Canadian province of Alberta, Grant Fuhr is the first black man to play goalie and win a Stanley Cup championship. During the 1987–88 season, Grant set an NHL record by winning 16 playoff games.

Championship banners soar over the Montreal Forum, the home arena of the Canadiens.

#7

Answer: The Montreal Canadiens. Montreal has won 23 championships, more than any other professional football, hockey, or basketball team. In 1996 the New York Yankees won their 23rd baseball championship, tying Montreal's record.

Vezina Trophy

Art Ross Trophy

Answer: The Vezina Trophy is given to the NHL's best goaltender each season. The goalie for the team with the fewest goals against in the regular season is awarded the trophy. It is named for Georges Vezina, one of hockey's earliest professional goalies who played in the 1890s. ***The Art Ross Trophy is given to the NHL player who scores the most points in a season.*** Art Ross was a former player and coach for the Boston Bruins.

Answer: 1.22. Divide Messier's points (1,468) into the games he has played (1,201). 1,468 divided by 1,201= 1.22129. Round this number out and you get 1.22. Any number over 1.00 is considered very good.

Answer: 2.78. First, multiply Patrick Roy's goals against (165) x 60. The answer is 9,900. Second, divide 9,900 by 3,565. Patrick Roy's goals against average is 2.7769. Round it up, and you get 2.78.

Patrick Roy

Joe Mullen

Answer: Joe Mullen of the Boston Bruins was born in New York City. In his NHL career, he has scored 495 goals and 546 assists. He is the highest scoring American to ever play in the National Hockey League and the only American to ever score more than 1,000 total points in his career. Joe has scored 1,041.

Resources to Check Out

Carrier, Roch. *The Hockey Sweater,* Trans. Sheila Fischman. Montreal, Quebec: Tundra Books, 1984.

McFarlane, Brian. *It Happened in Hockey.* Don Mills, Ontario: Stoddart Publishing Co., 1994.

McFarlane, Brian. *Proud Past, Bright Future, One Hundred Years of Canadian Women's Hockey.* Don Mills, Ontario: Stoddart Publishing Co., 1994.

Hunter, Douglas. *A Breed Apart: An Illustrated History of Goaltending.* Chicago: Triumph Books, 1995.

Terry Sawchuck makes a save.

Bibliography

Hunter, Douglas. *A Breed Apart, an Illustrated History of Goaltending.* New York: Viking Press, 1995.

Hockey: The Official Book of the Game. Hamlyn Press, 1990.

National Hockey League Stanley Cup Playoffs Fact Guide. Chicago: Triumph Books, 1995.

National Hockey League Official Guide and Record Book, 1996–1997. Chicago: Triumph Books, 1996.

McFarlane, Brian. *Proud Past, Bright Future: One Hundred Years of Canadian Women's Hockey.* Don Mills, Ontario: Stoddart Publishing Co., 1994.

Photo Credits

Photographs are reproduced with permission of: © Erich Lessing/Art Resource, N.Y., p. 6; Hockey Hall of Fame, pp. 8, 12, 15, 28, 30 (bottom), 49 (top), 54 (left); © ALLSPORT USA/Glenn Cratty, pp. 9, 21, 51; © ALLSPORT USA/Al Bello, pp. 16 (left), 54 (right); Bruce Bennett/BBS, pp. 16 (right), 39 (top left); Imperial Oil–Turofsky/Hockey Hall of Fame, pp. 17, 23, 50, 52 (bottom), 60; Mark Buckner, p. 18; SportsChrome East/West, Rich Kane, pp. 19 (top left); © ALLSPORT USA/Nevin Reid, p. 19 (top right); SportsChrome East/West, C. Melvin, pp. 19 (bottom left), 62; SportsChrome East/West, Scott Brinegar, p. 19 (bottom right); Quebec Nordiques, p. 26; © ALLSPORT USA/Elsa Hasch, p. 27 (top left); © ALLSPORT USA/Matthew Stockman, p. 27 (top right); © ALLSPORT USA/Robert Laberge, pp. 27 (bottom), 49 (bottom); University of Toronto Archives, p. 30 (top); From the Brian McFarlane Collection, p. 32; National Archives of Canada/PA 139440/With permission of The Molson Companies Limited, p. 33; SportsChrome East/West, Bongarts, Lutz Bongarts, p. 34; © ALLSPORT USA/Gray Mortimore, p. 35; SportsChrome East/West, Bongarts Photography, p. 36; SportsChrome East/West, Bongarts, A. Hassenstein, p. 37; © ALLSPORT USA/Craig Jones, p. 39 (top right); Frank Prazak/Hockey Hall of Fame, p. 39 (bottom left); © ALLSPORT USA/Rick Stewart, p. 39 (bottom right); Brantford Expositor, p. 42; © ALLSPORT USA/Nathaniel Butler, p. 44; © ALLSPORT USA/Brian Bahr, p. 47; SportsChrome East/West, Rob Tringali Jr., pp. 52 (top), 57; © North Wind Pictures, p. 55; © Richard B. Levine, p. 56; Doug MacLellan/Hockey Hall of Fame, p. 58 (both); ©ALLSPORT USA/Jamie Squire, p.59 (left) © ALLSPORT USA/Todd Warshaw, p.59 (right). Cover photograph from Imperial Oil–Turofsky/Hockey Hall of Fame.

African Americans, 22–27, 57
Art Ross Trophy, 58
assists, 38
Avercamp, Hendrick, 6

Bathgate, Andy, 12
Beckett, Henry, 22
Benedict, Clint, 15, 52
Brooks, Charles, 22

Carter, Anson, 26, 27
Cheevers, Gerry, 16

discrimination, 24, 26
Dominion Ladies Hockey Tournament, 33

Fuhr, Grant, 26, 27, 57

goalies, 13, 14, 15, 20, 34–35, 46
goals, 38
goals against average (GAA), 46
Graham, Elizabeth, 14
Granato, Cammi, 37
Gretzky, Wayne, 18, 40, 42, 43, 45, 49, 51
Grier, Mike, 26, 27
Guidolin, Bep, 53

Hextall, Ron, 20, 52, 55
history of hockey, 6–21, 28–31
hockey sticks, 12
Hoffman, Abby, 32
Howe, Gordie, 18, 42, 49, 51
Hull, Bobby, 17, 18
Hull, Brett, 18, 49

ice rinks, 9, 41, 56
International Hockey League, 13
International Ice Hockey Federation (IIHF), 33

James, Val, 24

Lemieux, Mario, 44, 49, 51, 56

masks, face, 13, 14, 15–16
McCallion, Hazel, 31
McKegney, Tony, 26
Messier, Mark, 44, 49, 51, 58
Montreal Canadiens, 57
Mullen, Joe, 59

nicknames, 17, 18, 50

Olympic Games, 36
O'Ree, Willie, 22–24

periods, 21
Plante, Jacques, 15–16, 18
players, number of, 7
plus-minus points, 45
points-per-game, 43
pucks, 8, 9, 10

referees, 11, 29
Rheaume, Manon, 34–35
Richard, Maurice, 17, 18
Roy, Patrick, 52, 59
rules, 8, 13, 29

Sakic, Joe, 38, 51
Sawchuck, Terry, 16
skates, ice, 55
Stanley Cup, 54
Stanley, Isobel, 29
Stanley, Lord and Lady, 28–29
statistics, 38–53; best goals against average in a single season, 52; fastest slapshot, 20; longest game, 25; most assists, 49; most goals scored, 49; most points per game, 51; most total points, 51; strangest game, 41

total points, 38

uniforms, 13, 16, 29, 30

Vanbiesbrouck, John, 46
Vezina Trophy, 58

whistles, 11
White, Alton, 24
Winter Landscape, 6
women, 14, 28–37

Zamboni machine, 56

About the Author

Bruce Adelson is a sports writer, substitute teacher, and former attorney whose published works include *The Minor League Baseball Book.* His work has also appeared in *The Four Sport Stadium Guide* and in publications such as *The Washington Post, Sport Magazine,* and *Baseball America.* The Sports Trivia books are his first children's publications. Adelson lives in Alexandria, Virginia.

About the Illustrator

Harry Pulver Jr. is an illustrator and animator who also plays the accordian and guitar. His work has appeared in numerous national ad campaigns and in books, including *Find It!* and *Tracking the Facts,* two other titles by Lerner Publications.